FAITH
HOPES
LOVE

Poems Inspiring...

Kathy,

My best
for your best.

J.K.

FAITH
HOPES

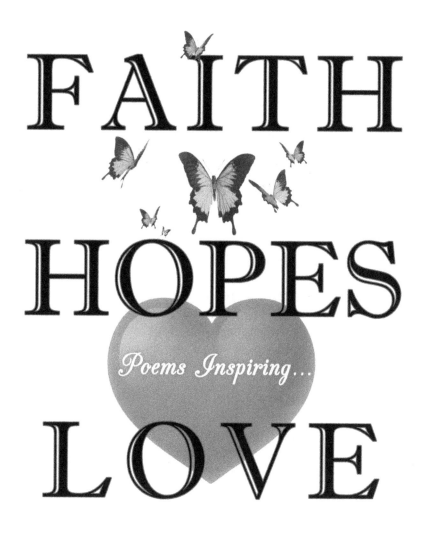

Poems Inspiring...

LOVE

J.K. Sandin

Illustrations by Grace Metzger Forrest

FAITH HOPES LOVE
Poems Inspiring ...

By J. K. Sandin

Paperback: ISBN: 978-1-943523-45-0

Mobi (Kindle): ISBN: 978-1-943523-46-7

ePub (Nook, iBooks): ISBN: 978-1-943523-47-4

Illustrations and Cover Design by Grace Metzger Forrest

Edited by Nancy E. Williams

Published by Laurus Books

LAURUS BOOKS
A DIVISION OF THE LAURUS COMPANY, INC.
www.TheLaurusCompany.com

This book may be purchased in paperback from TheLaurusCompany.com, Amazon.com, and other retailers around the world. Also available in formats for electronic readers from their respective stores.

DEDICATION

This volume of verse is dedicated to everyone for whom
faith is foundational, hope is fundamental, and
love is forever.

It has been said that faith is the substance of things hoped for,
as well as what evidences the yet unseen.
And what greater hope is there than to find a love
that will last forever, shared unconditionally
between two believing hearts.

This book is also dedicated to all who have loved me
in ways that have affirmed my faith and answered my hopes.
May all that you are believing for inspire a hope within,
fulfilled only by Love.

ACKNOWLEDGEMENTS

It is with sincerest gratitude of heart
that I acknowledge those who have taught me
all that I have come to understand and embrace of
faith and hope and love.

My God and Savior, Jesus Christ,
for being the love that has saved my soul.

My family of origin
for exemplifying both the love and grace that so nurtured me.

My relatives all
for embodying family values through your devotion to one another.

My friends all
for enriching my life through sharing many treasured times.

My pastors all
for enlightening me as to how faith in God is to be lived out daily.

My readers all
for encouraging me through being here to "hear" my heart singing.

TABLE OF CONTENTS

FOREWORD

FAITH HOPES LOVE: *Poems Inspiring ...*

is a universal experience of which this very project exemplifies. Writing has always been a passion for me but never manifested into anything more than a pleasurable pastime. Repeated comparisons of accomplished writers' noteworthiness to my own unworthiness made pipe dreams of my personal desires for authorship. And many times, I compromised my convictions by conceding to conditions of consequential ends: I would quit before I ever commenced writing. That is until now. My heart refused to be denied any longer. With faith arisen, this journey began.

Over the years, original poetic works had accumulated in my files with no one to read them. It took a long time before I dared to believe that my words were worth sharing with others. It no longer mattered to me how my voice compared to others. I simply needed for it to be "heard." With faith stirring inside me and hopes motivating me forward, I began compiling all of my musings into an anthology. Even though there appeared to be too few poems for a book, I was determined to see them all in print soon. And in my search for inspiration, I found the following ...

For now we see only a reflection as in a mirror; then we shall see face to face. Now I know in part; then I shall know fully, even as I am fully known. And now these three remain: faith, hope and love. But the greatest of these is love [1 Corinthians 13:12-13 NIV].

"Faith, hope, and love." This was the inspirational direction I needed for purposes of organizing everything into a presentable format. It would be a poetic story telling how faith creates the hope of eventually finding love. However, before I could share this universally appealing story, I needed to be completely convinced of my experience of it for myself. A story is only believable if its teller is fully persuaded of its veracity and impassioned to have it be told.

My belief in everyone being able to grasp this gave me hope that my story would become published. With more than enough material, there were only two things I lacked at that time: an illustrator and a publisher. This is where this my journey really gets interesting.

As I grew in faith, my increasingly compelling hopes prompted me to record the desires of my heart, and most importantly, as they related to what I believed in my soul. Namely, that my Divine destiny was to Love, and my life was to be experienced as being countless expressions of that love in all its facets and dimensions, both as a recipient and reservoir for it to flow in and through me to others. Awakened to this truth, and assured that everyone would likewise embrace this heart-stirring story, I sought out opportunities to share it. With more than enough content material, I only lacked an illustrator and a publisher. This is where my journey gets interesting.

A dear friend posted an announcement on on the internet about a book she was writing. Curious, I got in touch with her to find out more. That conversation resulted in a referral to a very reputable publisher who referred me to a most talented artist specializing in design and illustration work. I was most thankful for my good fortune, as I now lacked nothing in my dream becoming reality. It is in your hands now, thanks largely to the following people: Sharalee Sherman, who graciously provided me with the initial referral; Nancy E. Williams of The Laurus Company, who patiently guided me through every step of the publishing process; Grace Metzger-Forrest, who visually captured the essence of the story; Stephanie Freeman, who generously served as the model for the character in the story; and my sister, who willingly provided me with invaluable advice and support.

— James "J.K." Sandin

PREFACE

LIFE EMINATES FROM THE HEART, with attitudes and affirmations giving to life both virtues and validations. This giving fosters a purity of purpose, as if by a guiding grace, in all matters of faith for hope unto love. The language that best captures these fundamental truths in relationship to all things is poetry. It is the heart expressing ever after and always.

Words provide the details of dialogue in giving meaning to all messages. In poetry, the writer and reader intimately interact in a transcendence of communication. Hearts are mutually stirred by promptings to respond by believing, hoping, and loving. May this be descriptive of your experiences as you read the poetic story of "Faith Hopes Love."

INTRODUCTION

THIS VOLUME OF VERSE is appropriately titled "Faith Hopes Love," for that is the experiential discovery that it purposefully leads to through a poetically poignant and progressive story. Your heart will come to know the meaningfulness of the love for which Faith hopes as you journey with her in her search through the shared experiences outlined below.

H as in "HEARTS HEARING"
all that is present that intends for its attention.

E as in "HEARTS ENTERTAINING"
what attracts it for purposes of understanding.

A as in "HEARTS AFFIRMING"
what it now accepts and believes about everything.

R as in "HEARTS RELATING"
to others what is worth sharing out of its discoveries.

T as in "HEARTS TRUSTING"
what is treasured as true with that of another heart.

S as in "HEARTS SINGING"
over connections being made of "Faith, Hope, and Love."

The seventh section represents the musings of hearts, as personal discoveries often inspire poetic expressions capturing a deepened awareness of oneself and of life. Faith, hopes, and love are as essential to existence as are air, water, and space. How we prioritize, practice, and preserve them is what life is all about in essence. I liken "LIFE" to a continuation of everyone's unique "story."

Toward the end of this book, you will find in Appendix A a listing of every poem with its own back story. This is to ensure that you will know my heart in every poetic expression as well as the individual and collective relevance of the poems to the book and, more importantly, to your life. In Appendix B, you will find a listing of every illustration and the dramatized truth each one represents in the story.

Following the appendixes, you will find the Index, which includes an alphabetized listing of all the poems by their first lines. This will help you in conveniently locating the more than 100 original poems purposefully written, meaningfully crafted, and carefully placed in this volume of verse.

Faith Hopes Love is intended to be more than just a book to read and perhaps share with your friends and book club buddies. It is actually designed to be an experience of entertainment, enlightenment, and enrichment. Though the important subjects of faith, hope, love, and life are well presented in the poetic storytelling, graceful imagery, and intriguing perspectives, more was needed for this experience to be well remembered. That is why there is a special gift for you in the back of this book. It is a beautiful "LOVE Chart" rendition of 1 Corinthians 13:4-8 suitable for framing. Let it be an ever-present reminder that the love your heart hopes for can always be found through faith.

It is now our pleasure to present to you, *Faith Hopes Love: Poems Inspiring ...* Enjoy!

PROLOGUE

MY GREATEST DISCOVERIES have always been prompted by a compelling need to know. This is as consistently true as is the sun's rising and setting in preordained fashion. And, thus, here am I.

HEARING FAITH

In my being all that I'm becoming, I recall what someone once told me: "The extent to which truth resides in you is how true you can be with your world and connected with everyone in it." I took that to mean everyone including myself, perhaps the most difficult person of all to get to know. Then one day I distinctly felt a strong impression. It was like my soul was being pursued by an unrelenting force. Surrendering to it; I felt as if I was being drawn to the dawn. It soon dawned on me that I was in search of ... well ... me. And this journey was about to commence.

Nothing was going to either distract or deter me in this personal mission quest. Yet I was taken aback somewhat by the quietness of this purposefully contemplative time. It was as if nothing pre-existed this day. I was totally committed to spending every waking moment becoming better acquainted with me. It was about hearing what faith had to foretell my searching soul.

This process of deepening self-discovery was exhilarating to say the least. Even with the excited anticipation came a little unsettledness because of what the revelations might expose. Questions naturally arose in my mind. Will I hear clearly what's revealed to me in truth? Will I comprehend the significance of the likely changes brought on by

my expanded self-awareness? Will my resulting transformation posi-
tively or negatively affect my future in what will undoubtedly be my
new present? Before I could listen, I had to say no to some things first.

Silencing the cacophony of noises was more than just a matter of
escaping my external world, with its symphony of roaring engines
and resounding horns and crescendoing barks. It was also necessary
to suppress the clamoring of voiced thoughts from numerous origins,
with all replaying in my mind as if on a repeating loop. This took con-
siderable time and effort, but I was convinced that it would all be
worth it and, hopefully, soon. Too much depended on the success of
this venture. Finally, all things being momentarily well with my soul,
I reached for that one completely reliable source of truth for me: my
Bible. My answers were awaiting me there.

ENTERTAINING FAITH

Responding to a plethora of probative ponderings meant giving
serious consideration to each one. Having "heard" what I most needed
to hear, I was ready for entertaining these new inputs.

This next phase tested my confidence as to whether or not I had
the will to persevere in discovering the who, what, when, where, why,
and how of my identity. Answering this qualified me to proceed further
and deeper because real truths about oneself can be found neither on
the surfaces of things nor in sentiments of greetings. Accumulating
information does not make one knowledgeable any more than
acquiring books makes one scholarly. So my urgent interest was in
discerning the personal meanings of what came from those confiden-
tial contemplations.

As you can imagine, the questions came pouring into my heart.
They centered around what I was about and what there was about
me that was worth other people getting to know. An early and most
surprising discovery was that my self-concept had been based almost
entirely upon emotions: I am great or gross depending upon how I
was feeling at that particular moment. Another significant one was

that if I could not see it for myself, I would not believe it, especially if it was in regards to me. *Oh, ye of little faith, and much less common sense.* There was only one conclusion that could be reached: these revelations all needed to be addressed.

At that epiphanous juncture, another saying was recalled to mind: "Faith is the substance of things you hope for, as well as the evidence of things that go unseen." This was to be a guiding principle for me as I moved forward. The truth about me, as I reasoned, could be solid enough on which to anchor my beliefs and provided the means of disciplining feelings about life and myself.

A rediscovered personal journal became an enlisted aid for this critical mission. It was time for me to begin ascertaining the meaningfulness of what was becoming known to me about my true self. The arduously introspective self-examination of my soul quickly transformed information into insights. I came to understand why things were as they were (e.g., conditions and circumstances contributing to the creation of meaningless matters, methods, and means).

My thoughts, as well as my corresponding decisions and actions, were often impulsive reactions to needs and necessities and were seldom tempered by truth or guided by grace. The desire for everything would never lead me to a want of nothing but, rather, that of increasingly more still. Yet, being satisfied with these entertained truths and what they would do in and for me was not enough. I concluded then that my newly established perspectives, based on principles of fundamental faith, must be firmly committed to for purposes of preserving them in perpetuity.

AFFIRMING HOPES

I reasoned that repetition and redundancy make for routine and reinforcement. Though the concept of AFFIRMING was somewhat foreign to me, my heart demanded its practice.

It is always a challenge to rightly and accurately predict and prepare for what may be impending or improbable. I found myself unrelieved of the dilemma of having to respond to many disparate factors in my life. How could the mere recitation of well-intended words and cleverly composed phrases ever prove to be enough of a reply to any or all? What could come of such an exercising of the will, I wondered. Then it came to me. Just as there are colors that are descriptive of life, so too are there values constructive of life. With this in mind, I continued the promising process.

The most basic of all truths to declare about oneself seemed like a good place to start. And so it began, albeit awkwardly at first, but it soon became an edifying and empowering discipline ...

- *I am one of countless many, and never to be the lesser of any.*
- *I am worthy of love, respect, and regard as much as is anyone.*
- *I am made to be the head and not the tail, above and not beneath.*
- *Nothing shall be impossible for me with God, as He has promised.*
- *I can do all things through Christ who gives me strength.*
- *I am capable of all that I commit myself to doing and more.*
- *I will no longer stand in my way, but stand at all times for always.*

I oftened wondered what would come of all this soul searching and truth seeking. Affirming the changes happening within me was like forming a new self-image by using the building blocks of belief laid upon the firm foundation of affirmed Truth. This instilled in me something more valuable than anything tangible and more precious than anything treasured. For the first time in a very long while, I had genuine hope for permanent change and prosperous tomorrows. I felt truly blessed, but I could not keep this all to myself. And so progressively onward I went.

RELATING HOPES

The next step in this process of living more by faith and less by feelings—this was how I related to this experience—was to do the same on a broader scale by relating these changes to my world.

Knowing is good for the sake of being well informed and for making wise, educated decisions. However, that only begs the following question: "So what?" The benefits derived from hearing and entertaining faith and subsequently affirming renewed hopes were greatly appreciated indeed. But before me was the proverbial fork in the road. I could choose a new road to a hoped-for better destination, or more precisely, new destiny. The other direction would actually take me back to complacent contentment, a place I had spent much effort endeavoring to leave. I chose the alternative way.

Unfamiliarity normally breeds insecurity and intolerance, but not in my case. What was known beforehand, I had for all intents and purposes outgrown. Most needed at this time was further personal growth in this matured state of being. I wanted to witness for myself demonstrations of these changes as I related them to people, places, and things nearest to me, and eventually well beyond that to where only Providence knew. Like the old saying goes: put up or shut up.

In this phase of relating my hopes to others, it behooved me to approach my family before anyone else, as they would best be able to judge if and how I had changed by the way I related to them as my truer self. Seeing their delight over the new me was reassuring, as were their positive comments. This bolstered my resolve to live this out in relationship to everyone I knew, and with everyone I would chance meet in the places I would revisit, and in re-engaging myself with the things I used to do. The difference this time was my informed self-awareness emboldened an inspired self-confidence enhancing an ever increasing self-esteem. It was evident to all that my hopes were real and ready to reveal, but for what?

TRUSTING LOVE

Even with all of the personally gratifying interactions and exchanges experienced among those I related my hopes to, I was left with a disappointing sense of incompletion. So, what next?

Personal progress is never without its puzzle pieces. What my

5

heart intensely desired then was going unfulfilled. Unfortunately for me, an apparent missing piece to my hoped-for reality seemed lost. It had not fallen somewhere on the floor of my busy existence. Perhaps it was somehow misplaced, awaiting to be found in my box of treasured memories. In any event, something very significant was still out of the picture, and my heart was grieved over it.

Then, like a lighthouse beam shining over the sea, what I had not seen before suddenly became crystal clear to me. "Relating my heart" on more satisfying levels would require going even deeper. I pondered the means by which this could best be accomplished. Of course, it would have to be through trusting more of myself with another person. Relating *safely* from an emotional distance, relationally speaking, was choosing to remain in shallow depths of disclosure. I was wanting more ... and then the missing piece appeared. It was love.

Love is inherently elemental to life. Yet, it is what faith hopes for most in a searching soul. Trusting more substantively on an intimate heart-to-heart basis would inevitably create bonds between those who have entered into each other's places and spaces within. Who hopes for love––to love and be loved––is everyone who would have the faith to believe it were possible for him or her, and certainly for them. This took a quantum leap for me then, as it always has since. I risked my trust being violated if love were to have been denied me after having given it to another with all of my hopes therein contained. A full life demands this, and yet there is more.

SHARING LOVE

The pinnacle of self-worth was not simply being able to confidently trust my deepest truths with another person, as I had expected. It was and is *sharing love* unconditionally with everyone.

Heard through faith were the truths about myself revealed to me as I listened with my heart. *Entertained by faith* were these truths internalized in order to make them meaningful to me. *Affirmed hopes* were repeated declarations of personalized truths created for me.

Related hopes were the means by which I was able to purposefully connect myself to others.

Trusted were the deeper truths of myself that I came to know, to become bonded to another in love. I could not help but think there remained for me one final step before I could honestly say I had arrived at my desired destination:

> *To love as I am loved*
> *in being who I was predestined to be.*

No two stories are alike when it comes to personal growth journeys. This was a fact I could not take for granted as I opened myself further to love. Where I was then compared to where I had come from as a person of declared worth and claimed promise were assessments I could make of myself but not of others. It was incumbent upon me to accept people as they were in the moment and not prejudge them in any way. To have done so would have meant that love was not truly shared, and I was not authentically living love as I had professed. How was this to be done?

It was obvious to me where I needed to go for the answer to that question, and I found it in a familiar passage from an authoritative Source. Informative and convicting describe my experiences in reading these truths, with the former being obvious and the latter being surprising even to me. Rarely had I consciously considered the extent to which love motivated my thoughts, words, or actions. This is decidedly wrong, of course, as we always ought to be conscientious in how we treat ourselves as well as others. The enumerated characteristics of love listed on the next page were those my heart most earnestly desired to experientially know.

- Love is patient,

- love is kind.

- It does not envy,

- it does not boast,

- it is not proud.

- It does not dishonor others,

- it is not self-seeking,

- it is not easily angered,

- it keeps no record of wrongs.

- Love does not delight in evil but rejoices with the truth.

- It always protects, trusts, hopes, perseveres.

- Love never fails.

[1 Corinthians 13:4-8 NIV]

I end this account with what unquestionably is the greatest discovery of the heart: it is that love is only known when it is shared. And the real message of the story you are about to read is simply this:

Faith Hopes (in a God Who is) Love

SECTION ONE

Poems Inspiring ...

HEARTS
HEARING
FAITH

"Truths are awaiting discovery in the
quietness of contemplation,
and the heart knows this well."

BEING AND BECOMING

If I always could be who I could be,
there would be no need for dreaming.

If I always could be what I could be,
there would be no desire for aspiring.

If I always could be when I could be,
there would be no incentive for preparing.

If I always could be where I could be,
there would be no reason for planning.

If I always could be why I could be,
there would be no purpose for believing.

If I always could be how I could be,
there would be no motivation for learning.

Since I am as I am being,
there is always an authenticity for becoming.

I AM

I am who I am, not the image others project to me ...
as I imagine myself to be, I am.

I am what I am, not the help others want from me ...
as I help myself to be, I am.

I am when I am, not the expectations others hold for me ...
as I expect myself to be, I am.

I am where I am, not the position others associate with me ...
as I position myself to be, I am.

I am why I am, not the reason others decide about me ...
as I reason myself to be, I am.

I am how I am, not the judgment of others reached of me ...
as I judge myself to be, I am.

I am because I am, not the labels others place upon me ...
As I declare myself to be, I am.

THAT I MAY KNOW

Brokenness, that I may know strength,

Failure, that I may know success,

Grief, that I may know recovery,

Injury, that I may know healing,

Loss, that I may know gain,

Fear, that I may know peace,

Rejection, that I may know acceptance,

Bible, that I may know God,

Jesus, that I may know Love,

Spirit, that I may know Truth,

Church, that I may know worship,

Family, that I may know belonging,

Friendship, that I may know you,

Life, that I may know me.

ALL THINGS BE

To be peaceful, I'll seek peace.

To be happy, I'll share happiness.

To be respected, I'll show respect.

To be thankful, I'll offer thanks.

To be faithful, I'll live faith.

To be hopeful, I'll inspire hope.

To be lovable, I'll freely love.

To be all things, I shall all things be.

LIKE THIS IS THAT

Like a snow-capped peak, this fresh perspective

is learning by heart that acquires new visions.

Like a day's dawning, this revealing paradigm

is listening with heart that applies new insights.

Like a cloudless sky, this clarifying truth

is loving in heart that affirms new convictions.

Like a distant horizon, this vastness of time

is living from heart that actualizes new delights.

Poems Inspiring…

HEARTS
ENTERTAINING
FAITH

"A heart must be discerning
of what has entered it, and
whether it should remain."

WHY ...

... do we hate one another for the cause of race,

denying, dividing, disrespecting due to skin.

... do we lie (to) one another in the pursuit of place,

scheming, shading, and sensationalizing to spin.

... do we fight one another at a party's embrace,

misrepresenting, misquoting, and misinforming to win.

... not love one another, then, as in providing space,

affirmingly, admiringly, and affectionately from within.

... not speak truth (to) one another, then, as in revealing face,

humbly, honorably, and holily from herein.

... not give (to) one another, then, as in saving grace,

characteristically, charitably, and cheerfully to wherein.

IN WANT OF NOTHING

A stormy night cannot thwart peacefulness from prevailing.

A critical comment cannot keep causes from proving just.

A laughter long silenced cannot restrain joy from returning.

A mistake committed cannot preempt Jesus from restoring trust.

A song without lyrics cannot stop hearts from singing.

A cloud-filled sky cannot keep hope from shining through.

A vision long forgotten cannot deter dreams from being.

A door firmly closed cannot prevent God from blessing you.

LOVE IS ...

The smile in the eyes of a person you hold dear,

and the pleasure from being in their heart.

The laughter of children while opening their gifts,

and the delight derived from their happiness.

The reason a young puppy leaps upon your lap,

and a kitten nuzzles with a comforting purr.

The sun's warmth upon your face each morning,

and the moon's glow calling you to rest.

The comfort of a departed soul's remembrance,

and the benefaction gratefully embraced.

The applause of an audience being entertained,

and the performer's bows in appreciation.

The gratitude of a stranger who once was in need,

and your heart's delight after giving him hope.

The security in knowing, "It is well with my soul,"

and the assurance of faith that God makes it so.

WHEN COMES TWO HEARTS IN ONE

Love persuading, my affirmations assessed
of grace sufficing, my convictions confessed.

Heart compelling, my lofty interests inspired
by truth illuminating, my real destiny desired.

Commencing the Spring of my hopes unfolding
what awakens within this man's heart holding.

Calling softly within me, like a sweet warmth welcoming
dreams driving expectancy, the happiest homecoming.

Beautiful our minds, like invitations to passions prevailing
upon our harmonies to foretell of an unimaginable unveiling.

The will of a Father for His children in beneficent believing
having their hearts united in highest aspirations achieving.

ALWAYS

In secret I would wonder much

of happiness, success, and such.

Like shimmering stars so far away

beyond my reach, yet I would pray,

"Oh, gracious God, as You so will,

bless my life and desires fulfill."

Very soon after as I had believed,

love has arisen, of heaven received.

Exceeding all hopes is this delight,

one which inspires my heart aflight.

Yearning and longing for love's embrace,

discovering it showing through Your face.

"Oh, glorious Father, I know it is true.

This special blessing has come from You."

"Unto You, O God, your praise I extol,

with love overflowing my joyful soul."

Poems Inspiring...

HEARTS
AFFIRMING
HOPES

"The heart declares
something as truth when it validates it
through a devoted adherence."

WHAT COMES OF HOPE

Demands in life are like tales timely tested.

Dreams of life are like stories subconsciously savored.

Decisions in life are like narratives notably nested.

Desires for life are like findings fashion favored.

Longing, the languishing years turn into nows.

Listening, the lingering moments return timeless.

Laughing, the lyrical melody turns wondrous the wows.

Loving, the largesse my hope turning me speechless.

IN WANT I WONDER (Part 1)

Night welcomes the hope of morning

Where dreams and promises abide.

The choice, what fantasy imagines, or

Follow my heart as guide.

This journey starts with horizons vast,

And stayed by wisdom earned.

No longer bound by failures past,

For toward success I turn.

Before me awaits a future bright,

Giving shall thus I receive.

With want of opportunity no more,

I am as I believe.

MY HEART ALL WAYS

Unto the cause of grace, it expresses.

Unto the cause of Truth, it confesses.

Unto the cause of faith, it professes.

My heart (believes) all ways.

On the path of righteousness, it pursues.

On the path of holiness, it ensues.

On the path of promise, it renews.

My heart (hopes) all ways.

For the sake of joy, it beholds.

For the sake of peace, it enfolds.

For the sake of all, it upholds.

My heart (loves) all ways.

MY LOVE IS ...

Gracious, like a balm that soothingly restores
the aroma of lilies savoring to the soul.

Uplifting, like a wind that increasingly raises
the heights of imagination enriching to the mind.

Nurturing, like a song that harmoniously resonates
the lyrics of love enthralling to the spirit.

Beautiful, like a painting that captivatingly romances
the visions of beauty delighting to the heart.

THE WAYS TO YOU

Dream,

as the recreation of desire,

Foretells what awaits

the longing heart.

Faith,

as the reception of forever,

Believes what inspires

the everlasting spirit.

Hope,

as the reflection of harbor,

Summons what recalls

the sheltering soul.

Love,

as the revelation of life,

Embraces what beholds

the captivating form.

Poems Inspiring...

HEARTS
RELATING
HOPES

"The heart knows that convictions
are meaningful and made relevant
through interactions."

THINKING OF YOU

Beautiful as an incomparable jewel, and I am ... Jubilant.

Radiant as an iridescent morning, and I am ... Awakened.

Engaging as an intimate touch, and I am ... Mesmerized.

Novel as an inspired creation, and I am ... Enriched.

Desirable as an insatiable hunger, and I am ... Surrendered.

Altogether as an inhabited blessing, and I am yours ... Always.

FLOWING ...

... like a wind uplifting dreams,
making what seemed impossible and impractical
a transformed promised probability.
... like a river moving
the desires so long withheld from others' view,
now transported.
... like a beam of light illuminating
what could be still out of a darkened deceit
of what has not been: the triumph of truth.
... like a blood stream enlivening
the entire body, promoting health and vitality
for the joys of living in the generosity of grace.
... like a highway crisscrossing
making acquaintance with new vistas
of experience-expanding perspectives.
... like a thought inspiring,
changing the directions of aspiration and ambition
to the places where our hearts hold hope.
... like a well-crafted expression,
though inadequate in satisfaction, speaks
what I feel for you: limitless luxuriant love.

MUSICAL ROSES:
ALL THAT SUPPOSES

Musical roses from faith gardening dreams.

Flourishing harmonies which hopeful hearts sing.

Blossoming movements from love's unfolding themes.

Ornamenting rhapsodies that Divine blessings bring.

Savored bouquets from the gathering of thoughts.

Rendered arrangements just as pleasuring to show.

Presented endearments from care unendingly sought.

Composed selections of musings being mine to bestow.

FROM A MAN'S DESIRE ...

By Spirit to spirit is heaven shown.

For a man's soul is Truth sung.

Into a man's life is virtue sown.

From a man's heart is love sprung.

... OF A WOMAN'S HEART

My eyes, delighting you with fond attendance.

My hands, warming you with tender caresses.

My arms, enveloping you with sweet assurance.

My lips, arousing you with passion's kisses.

LOVE FOLLOWS
THE LONGING HEART

Searching for the treasure that far exceeds all riches,

Exploring at lengths, depths, and heights, either large or small.

Examining who, what, and where in the process of encounter,

Discovering the journey itself makes urgent a heart's call.

Listening is a heart aware of the calling from another,

Observing a figure nearing what it longs to behold.

Valuing the person now in passion's resolute pursuit,

Experiencing delights in togetherness as its stories unfold.

Wondering the answers why two would walk not as one,

Identifying fears that undermine a faith that ever guides.

Learning how once upon a time has become undeniably true,

Leaving past passed, our hearts are where our love resides.

Poems Inspiring...

HEARTS
TRUSTING
LOVE

"When hopes become portals
for love to flow through,
the heart reaches out in trust."

TOGETHERING

There are times, chance we, when what can be

is in our choices best.

And they come, we know, from far and fro;

treasures of hearts at quest.

Not by ways, or things, or want of kings,

but blessings nonetheless.

As we dared, believed so, received on we go,

faithful to Love's behest.

OUR JOURNEY FROM THEN

(CONNECTING)

Quiet is the night, deep is the silence,
and my heart stirs with thoughts of you.

Slow are the hours, long are the moments,
and my mind awakens with dreams in view.

Speak the sweet vision, here in the now,
and your voice sings my soul's reprise.

Laugh, the free spirit, smiles in the air,
and your presence holds my heart's surprise.

Vast the days appear, horizons in the light,
and our words drawing us closer together.

Talk as the melody, unison in the song,
and our passions bringing us into each other.

OUR JOURNEY TO WHEN

(SUMMONING)

Life's path known, a detour emerges,

and to what is from what must be.

Choice leads there, my heart recognizes,

and a voice beckoning, "Talk to me."

Desire's part shown, a call reveals,

and two souls seeking a connection true.

Openly shared feelings, thoughts, beliefs declared,

and we reach to touch what shall ensue.

Journey's distant tone, a sound announces,

and we are together in spirit and bound in peace.

Joining in being, joys in the flow,

and embracing each other as we live the increase.

OUR JOURNEY AND AMEN

(DESIRING)

Often now I wonder, what is happening to me,

and you summon, and defenseless I am rendered.

Yet, amazed am I, warm breezes in the winter,

and you are all I want, and I have entered.

Once was I free, the child with fearless wings,

and feeling now the unseen weights of life falling.

At night I embrace you, angel of moments' delights,

and sensing pleasure over you and my heart's calling.

Would that I could see, the view of angels abiding near,

and the next nows they reserve for our keeping.

No vision so desirous, images arousing my soul,

as you and I sow into a love's reaping.

IN WANT I WONDER (PART 2)

Before me now is beauty rare,

Beyond what memory has seen.

Extending my hand, I long to touch

What faith and happiness can bring.

No distance too far to travel,

And nothing left to test.

I answer what calls from deep within:

My desiring heart's behest.

In approaching I no longer wonder,

"Is it too good to be true?"

And the thought that prospers hope

Is the want of knowing you.

Poems Inspiring...

HEARTS
SHARING
LOVE

"The heart feels the joys
that love inspires and
enthusiastically joins in the sharing."

MY THOUGHTS OF YOU

Time passes slowly as the distance narrows,

My heart's longing for where a friend awaits.

Hope arises fully as the anticipation grows,

My mind's musing from cherished portraits.

Desire stirs strongly as kept emotion flows,

My being's experiencing what passion creates.

Dreams come truly as you finally appear,

My eyes beholding more beauty then imagined.

Smiles greet warmly as you slowly draw near,

My soul's moving by an inspiration awakened.

Love felt sincerely as you embrace me so dear,

My spirit's rejoicing over wishes being answered.

MY LOVE IS HOME

Forever and a day my heart searches

Love in the horizon of time.

Carried by the wind are whispered sounds

Flowing in the rhythm of rhyme.

Awakened now, my arms outstretched,

Desire in the destiny of embrace.

Driven as if compelled by hope

Held in the providence of grace.

Arriving the day often visited in dreams,

Pleasure in a library of tome.

New firsts unfolding upon the discovery,

You are the embodiment of home.

OUR LOVE IS LIKE

Like the fragrance of flowers in pleasuring presence,

and he is titillating to my senses.

Like the welcomeness of wonderful in delighting desire,

and she is appealing to my sight.

Like the sweetness of surprise in engrossing enchantment,

and he is delicious to my savoring.

Like the reverence of revelation in favoring faith,

and she is heavenly to my soul.

Like the blessedness of beauty in deepening devotion,

and he is adorable to my surrender.

YESTERDAYS' TOMORROWS

Yesterdays' tomorrows, as blessings follow

Our hearts and minds in Thine.

Each today, by faith always,

We search for love Divine.

At last, we look past

Holding hope in our hands.

Losses gone, we carry on,

Daydreaming "what if" plans.

What is hers and his,

Shared in the flows of time

Every night, now in sight,

Love in graphic arts rhyme.

EVER VALENTINES

Your loveliness is as stunning as the clearest diamond.

Your embraces are as soothing as the calmest stream.

Your thoughts are as searching as the cleverest detective.

Your passions are as satisfying as the choicest dream.

My wishing of attraction is greeted in your appearance.

My wanting for affection is gratified through your caress.

My warming to consideration is groomed by your wisdom.

My welcoming in satisfaction is granted from your largess.

"The heart feels the joy that love inspires and enthusiastically joins in the sharing."

58

HEARTS

Thank you for taking the time to read the story of "Faith Hopes Love," poetically presented with the beautiful artistry of Grace Metzger-Forrest. This special project was actually inspired by a poem I wrote over 30 years ago on finding a love hoped for through faith: "The Dawning of Christmas." As an expression of my appreciation to you, I have added the rest of my poetic verses for your further reading pleasure:

"Hearts Musing Life"

The heart was divinely conceived and created for the highest possible purpose: to love and be loved. Life is the journey through which we move ever onward in realizing personal fulfillment of that purposefulness for living. When so fortunate, love occurs quite often indeed. It's why hope rises up whenever the very word is spoken, as in the phrase "I love you." Awareness of the hope-filled heart is an awakening to what awaits it, though where?

Don't let your heart be swayed into settling for counterfeits to love. You'll recognize them for the ease in which they were found by you, as if a trap had been set to ensnare your soul. The temptation of experiencing instant gratification of strong personal urges or immediate satisfaction of long-denied desires, can lead you away by your

senses from what is purposed about you. Faith is the key to appre-
hending what's hoped for in love: fulfillment.

What fulfills is by nature and necessity something that does not
need anything more than itself in order to achieve its intentions. This
can only be said about love. Love is of God, but more importantly than
that, God Himself is Love. Therefore, your purpose, the reason for
your being created, can only be realized and fulfilled by and through
God. This is the true meaning of the "Faith Hopes Love" story. Hear
this truth from wiser words taken from the Holy Bible:

*"Whoever does not love does not know God, because GOD IS LOVE.
This is how God showed his love among us: He sent his one and only Son
into the world that we might live through him. This is love: not that we
loved God, but that he loved us and sent his Son as an atoning sacrifice
for our sins...And so we know and rely on the love God has for us. GOD
IS LOVE. Whoever lives in love lives in God, and God in them."* [1 John
4:8-10, 16]

It is my wish for you, if you have not experienced this already, that
what your heart hopes for most will be realized and fulfilled through
faith in the One by whom Love has come: God in Christ Jesus. Amen.

God bless,
James "J.K." Sandin

SECTION TWO

Poems Inspiring...

HEARTS
MUSING
LIFE

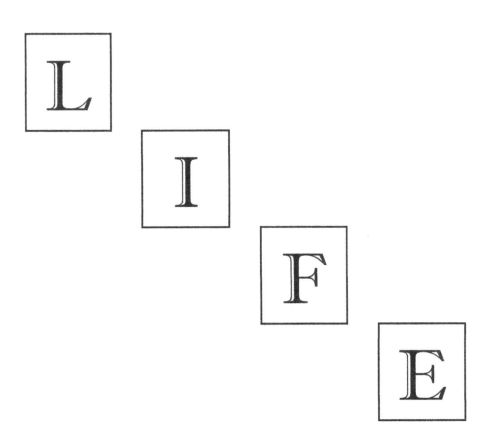

**"The heart is like life,
enlarging with every experience and
extending with every embrace."**

A BRIDGE COVERS THEIR HEART

Masterfully constructed an everlasting hope,

Steadfastly chronicling generations gone by.

Memories etched on old protective beams,

Love's opportunity to endearingly testify.

Among those sheltered a message reads,

"Jim & Karen, Ever & Always, 2005".

Occupying a place spanning what has begun,

Extending to what remains ever true...

A Bridge Covers Their Heart

A CANDLE IN THE HEART

A MOTHER'S LOVE IS LIKE ...

A soothing warmth and in its glow

A revealing light as it can show

A calming peace by which you know

A binding truth to wit shall grow

A living faith and from it bestow

... A CANDLE IN THE HEART.

A CHILD YEARNS
FOR WHAT A HEART RETURNS

Hunger is for a child what pain is for a fall:
emptiness and grief in an absence of relief.
Thirst is for a child what parched is for a pall:
intensely desired in a search uninquired.

Want is for a child what lack is for a hole:
needing voice in a poverty of choice.
Alone is for a child what gone is for a soul:
living lonely in a oneness of only.

Food is from the heart what fills from the more:
nourishment thriving as a fuel for driving.
Drink is from the heart what springs from the pour:
refreshment sustaining as a more thus gaining.

Plenty is from the heart what comes from the behest:
satisfaction achieving as a faith now believing.
Love is from the heart what derives from the best:
affection embracing as a heaven comes gracing.

A MOTHER'S LOVE

More beautiful than a rose in full bloom.

More valuable than all the world's wealth.

More precious than a newborn baby's face.

More enduring than even time itself.

More dependable than the sun that rises.

More incomparable than anything treasured.

More faithful than the dearest neighbor.

More giving than what can ever be measured.

The greatest gift after eternal salvation.

Divinely ordained, inspired, and true.

Hoping, nurturing, forgiving, believing.

More glorious in its reflection of you.

A SPECIAL SOMEONE

Faced with worry and trouble, problems everywhere.
I can't seem to cope with them, it's like I just don't care.
Trying to find the answers, often being unable to see.
The problems growing larger, to the point of blinding me.

I've met a special person, one who's gentle and kind.
A heart both joyous and loving, a type impossible to find.
In appearing before me quickly, I soon became aware.
God, you provided her for me, like an answer to a prayer.

These times spent together, they're important indeed.
Sharing our pains and sorrows, understanding of this need
No longer do I feel lonely, depression and fear are gone.
My world is once again beautiful, with gratitude I carry on.

In all these precious moments, a newfound love is come.
There's absolutely never a doubt, I know full well wherefrom.
I can't thank Him enough, everything for which He's done.
Showing me my Special Someone, for accepting me as His son.

A TEACHER NEVER RETIRES

Gone are the days of early risings,
Waiting on buses, and chasing down kids.
Of planning lessons, and self-sacrificings.
No more IEPs, oh, God forbid.

As I awaken, each morning pleases.
My time for all time is mine.
Moments enjoyed as life now eases
Into works of my own design.

To family and friends I give my attention.
Visiting people and places for things.
Needing and doing as I plan direction.
Such is the life that retirement brings.

Looking back from once looking forward,
I discover a truth that truly inspires.
From lifelong instructing comes this regard:
By nature and nurture no teacher retires.

A TEACHER'S PRAYER

God, what now seems a lifetime ago,

You spoke to my heart and let me know

as for my life You were calling me

to care for those so few could see.

Beyond being special as they are,

their joy to me was greater by far.

I spent my life at Your behest;

giving to them my heart, my best.

Reflecting now, to this I was true:

their highest good was mine to pursue.

About me may they remember thus:

their quality of life was always first, plus

giving whatever I could possibly give,

I entrusted them all to You to live

a better life through faith by grace,

and in my eyes behold your face. Amen.

ADDING CHANGES

Read becomes bread, as if by magic,

but if it's dread, how sad and tragic.

What must be done,

by all if not one?

Think with your head, that is the trick.

Art may be smart, if not also strange.

It can be marts, should you rearrange.

As to what is,

true if true 'tis.

Believe all not part: add leads to change.

ALWAYS MY VALENTINE

I feel you, yet never having touched you.

I see you, yet never having beheld your beauty.

I know you, yet never having met you.

I desire you, yet never having embraced your essence.

Would that time and distance be passages to bliss.

and my body and heart be yours in a kiss.

Would that dreams and fantasies be real by design,

and my heart's desire be always my valentine.

AN END'S BEGINNING

Is it true that true it is?

Be it could if could it be?

Not I know is know I not.

See to some as some to see.

Come over now to now overcome.

Turn around then or then around turn.

That was there for there was that.

Begin to end thus end to begin.

AS IS MY LADY TO ME

Heaven, as the glory of grace,

is the Magnificence of your soul.

Adoration, as the declaration of devotion,

is the Yearning of your spirit.

Truth, as the clarity of conscience,

is the Loyalty of your heart.

Talent, as the presentation of promise,

is the Agency of your blessing.

Inspiration, as the quintessence of quest,

is the Designing of your destiny.

Excellence, as the aspiration of achievement,

is the Yielding of your life.

AT LONG LAST LOVERS

The heart longs for the one who graces dreams,

inhabiting thoughts visualized in night visitations.

Unaware the longings another heart embraces,

inclining lives destined in Divine preparations.

There are times when the heart demands action,

inspiring hopes purposed in active searches.

Options are many in choosing where to focus,

including sites preferred in dating urges.

Overwhelmed by the vast number of searchers,

inquiring minds expressed in personal passions.

Understanding the key to making a connection,

inspiring words presented in favorable fashion.

Available for viewing is the messaging of "me",

interesting profiles composed in liberal language.

Doubts from the past leave, as greetings are sent,

inviting response received, in willingness engage.

(continued on next page)

76

AT LONG LAST LOVERS Cont.

The heart risks all when its desires are awakened,
investing hours bonded in sweet repose.
Meaningful is the mutuality of revealed emotions,
intimating loves professed in truth arose.

What naturally follows as hearts set their courses,
initiating plans imagined in fondest dreams.
Decisions acted upon in the fulfilling of promises,
intending vows validated in favored themes.

Lovers at long last becoming united as one,
invoking grace imparted in always ever.
Continually celebrating this blessed and gifted life,
integrating what's predestined in Love forever.

BEING GOOD FOR BETTER TO BEST

Being good

Seeking good

Finding good

Sharing good

Becoming better for goodness sake.

Being better

Seeking better

Finding better

Sharing better

Becoming best for betterment sake.

Being best

Seeking best

Finding best

Sharing best

Being what's sought, found, and shared.

BUT WE SEE JESUS

Rioting in the streets of our nation,

Arguing which lives matter more.

Lootings belying the calls for liberation,

Stirring up hatred evens the score.

But we see Jesus.

Shootings of the masses in such savaged guile,

Terrorizing hope like the onslaught of disease.

Slaughtering the peace as prescribed by denial,

Attacking resolution as fears and evils seize.

But we see Jesus.

Abusing drugs and people with violent notions,

Destroying potentials such habits inflame.

Sacrificing lives in the deadliness of proportions,

Inviting fatalistic guilt as punishment in shame.

But we see Jesus.

Recognizing how far we have fallen from grace,

Acknowledging that only God can truly save.

Confessing our sinfulness for mercy to embrace,

Repenting as trusting the One who forgave.

By thus we see Jesus.

CHRISTMAS DAWNS

First on my list was a church: recalling what I've known.

Where else but in a service: to hear, see, be shown.

Many were there singing loudly: some kneeling to pray.

It was as I expected: same questions with dismay.

Continuing on with the search: for what I wasn't sure.

Bible schools must have answers: knowledge to procure.

Students all busily learning: teachers expositing thoughts.

Lengthy discourses on Jesus: finding what I forgot.

Next on my list a mission: perhaps there's a piece.

A puzzle without a picture: my search may never cease.

People are all milling about: here, there, everywhere.

Jesus at every forefront: grace to have and share.

A homeless shelter is near: helping poor and needy.

Feeding, clothing, cleaning too: slick from the seedy.

With workman like precision: volunteering thrives.

Doing all that they can do: keeping all alive.

(continued on next page)

CHRISTMAS DAWNS Cont.

A crowd is forming elsewhere: a funeral to commence.

Approaching nonchalantly: not one aware of my presence.

A dirge is playing at the start: a preacher now walks in.

"Life, death, and eternity: you must be born-again."

Entering my neighborhood: everyone knows everyone.

Discouraged but still searching: I'll finish what I've begun.

Adults are watching children: families within a family.

Love binding hearts to each other: closer to my key.

Proceeding with my neighbors: of them two to wed.

Such joyous celebrating: to the truth ahead.

The vows so sweetly spoken: do they, yes they do.

The preacher gives the blessing: nice but nothing new.

So off to visit a friend: angel to the captives.

He to whom much was given: freely to all he gives.

Listening to what he's sharing: demonstrations of love.

Hearing these men responding: to heaven from above.

(continued on next page)

CHRISTMAS DAWNS Cont.

Leaving, I'm drawing closer: it'll come eventually.

Like those back in Bible times: light my Galilee.

In a hospice now to listen: to those nearing ends.

Hearing how they call on Jesus: I now comprehend.

Salvation is near to all: call upon His name.

There was still something missing: I still seem the same.

What motivates witnessing: seeing Who can't be seen?

Loving the unlovable: I'm betwixt and between.

Family is where I belong now: on to hearth and home.

What is it I'm to find there: the end of my roam?

Mom, dad, sister, brother: look so different now.

Could it be I SEE JESUS: through all I see Thou.

But for the gift of Jesus: Christmas would be naught.

Yet for the work of Jesus: heaven has been begot.

Christmas need not come to us only once a year.

Christmas dawns on you and me whenever Christ is near.

COME-UNITY

What's commonplace becomes complacency's companion.
The familiar that breeds contempt isn't an exception to this.
Habitually keeping reality-distorting rose-colored glasses on
Makes possible the oversimplifying of all things thought amiss.

What if we were to refrain from thoughts that inevitably end
With taking for granted the very means of enriching us all.
By such restraint beliefs would change and hopes transcend
Into a determined destiny that satisfies all rationale of the real.

So turn your hearts toward mine, and I shall do the same,
For creating community is a commitment of coming to unite.
Differences, diversities, and everything else that one can name
Are worth the embracing simply by virtue of the fact it's right.

Ask yourself a simple question to test your heart's resolve:
"Why should I stand alone when I could stand with you?"
Two may be better than one, but more are best to involve.
Being in community is knowing how to thine own self be true.

COMING ATTRACTIONS:
LIFE ON THE REAL SCREEN

Of course, the saga continues.

Viewer discretion is advised.

It will both amaze and amuse.

You're certain to be surprised.

And when that seems to be through,

Something unexpectedly happens.

A new coming attraction preview,

You can't wait for the day it opens.

Does this sound remotely familiar?

Is life full of episodes and sequels?

A little drama, suspense, or satire?

You're the writer; what's there to tell?

Stories and more stories we've all seen.

And despite this, one thing remains true.

The portal into your life is like a screen;

Always and evermore controlled by you.

CONTEXTING

What a CWOT that was.
B3 was all that I heard.
IDK and IDC because
BY&M that's NMP. Word!

Since that's SEP, I'll be fine.
And B4YKI, it'll all be done.
So BTAM, it's no longer mine.
NTIM, but soon I'll be gone.

Yes, giving PROPS is very good.
B4 I go, this I'll do only for you.
THX, and I'll behave as I should.
OMW now, to myself I'll be true.

It used to be so much easier to talk.
Words back then never had a next.
Knowing this makes it easier to walk
Together in a completely clear context.

CONFUSION'S INTRUSIONS

Wonder Blunder

Everything that's known was at one time shown.

What's discovered had to first be uncovered.

One seeks to find what's conceived in one's mind.

If not careful, to wonder may lead to blunder.

Analysis Paralysis

Once the item sought is found, it will come around.

A need to examine anything that leads to more.

It's not so easy to define each and every guideline.

If not careful, the analysis could cause a paralysis.

Fusion Delusion

Accumulation of facts is the very thing that distracts.

Making sense of the merged is what's most urged.

What happens in haste could make knowledge waste.

If not careful, the fusion could result in a delusion.

Inducive Conclusive

Everything may not be done if answers are few or none.

It all depends on how they come, as many or as some.

What's more important knowing is what will be showing.

If not careful, the inductive determines the conclusive.

DAD RHYMES WITH

RAD: being the coolest in my mind.

FAD: showing me he is one of a kind.

MAD: driving me crazy all of the time.

GLAD: having an attitude that was sublime.

BAD: never giving me any cause for concern.

GRAD: exhibiting in life a great capacity to learn.

GALIHAD: likened his pure nobility of character.

SINBAD: likened his great spirit of adventure.

IRONCLAD: aptly described the veracity of his soul.

COMRADE: finding the good in all always his goal.

SAD: leaving me a legacy dutifully to respect.

ADD: realizing for me he was my dad perfect.

DAWNINGS OF AGO

Memories, once the hopes of sought after futures,

become the dreams in reality's reflections.

Forward to present are the nuances for now;

hindsights gleaned from pasts' projections.

Influences complete like daybreak-filled skies,

raise new questions of what now from when.

Present from backwards are the yields of yore;

insights learned from ago and again.

FAITH, HOPE, AND LOVE:
A POEM

It's faith to believe that what's unseen

is still quite real indeed.

So here's the deal; you always kneel

in request, if not to plead.

From there you rise for certain wise,

the substance of your hope

Is meant to be as you'll undoubtedly see

a journey Divine is scope.

As truth appears what becomes quite clear,

it's never for you alone,

For in matters of grace, despite the race,

love is always to be sewn.

Why dare we fight and curse the night;

is that what's to be sought?

Pray be led through peace instead,

and by faith, hope, and love be taught.

FAMILY TIES

A family of four, and twice two more

has meant always the world to me.

What was then true, now as I knew

through it come blessings from Thee.

The dad as head of house and home.

The mom as heart of all therein.

The kids as hope of future's portent.

The grands as hands of love again.

What is this thing so closely knit

that binds lives by a grace supplied.

No chord so strong, no peace so great.

It's God Who creates all family ties.

GIVING VOICE TO GLORY

Veneration of Christ:

His worship as the breathing of my spirit,

and I am given to vocalize my sacrifices of praise.

Obedience to Christ:

His commands as the beckoning of my soul,

and I am called to oracle God's revelations in song.

Identification with Christ:

His life as the binding of my heart,

and I am moved to interpret God's Word and ways.

Conformation in Christ:

His likeness as the befitting of my mind,

and I am anointed to convince all need come along.

Exaltation through Christ:

His work as the bequeathing of my being,

and I am quickened to extol His name endless days.

GOODBYES BY GOOD

You can never bring back the past;
Or so they would have you believe.
It's not so much the dye was cast,
But what's there for you to receive.

There are always endings in a life:
Innocence of childhood, joys of youth,
Growths of adulthood, times of twilight.
But what's all the striving for: the truth!

There's nothing good in any goodbye,
Unless what's said needs nothing more.
When memories are sweet to the sigh,
Then the good created is yours to savor.

How we leave is important indeed,
And it's never wise to never look back.
Follow for yourself this simple creed:
Living for love never leads to lack.

GROOMING FOR BLOOMING

Why am I going through all of this pain?
What purpose is there to drown in the rain?
How can I avoid the unpleasantness here?
When will it end, and will I ever get there?

Where do I go to reclaim what's left of hope?
Who can I call upon when it's hard to cope?
I know what faith would have me to believe:
Pray to stay, and my heart's desires receive.

It's neither an issue concerning what I feel,
Nor about what I imagine is probably real.
I choose to confirm all matters by God's Word,
And live according to what my spirit has heard.

I'm a work in progress. My process, God's ways.
His blessings prompt me to offer Him praise.
Knowing He's grooming me for what is more;
This blossoming is all part of what is in store.

HELLO GOODBYES

Life is a series of starts and stops,

Comings and goings, or flips and flops,

Until everything reaches its end.

Too late to protect, preserve, or pretend.

Why say goodbye and suffer the pain,

Or say hello when all is in vain?

Life is a journey of doing one's best,

Greeting the moments as having been blessed.

HER WORDS, MY SOUL'S CARESS

Busy the days as time unfolds,

The cost of life's intent.

When need calls the mind to task,

At never a moment's relent.

Then in repose a voice is heard,

My world now calmly rests.

For soft my love abides in me,

Her words, my soul's caress.

HERE

You can't hold on to what is gone.

Nor can you see what's yet to be.

Embrace the wow that's in the now.

And remain aware while you're there.

IN ALL THINGS

What's in all things is conjecture's query.
There's both the obvious and the uncertain.
It's not mysterious so as to be eerie.
That's the reason to look at it again.

Nothing is really no thing, truth be told.
The curiosities of life lead to discoveries.
As what exists within begins to unfold,
Everything is every thing that may please.

A wise man once wrote on this issue
In a letter to a People universal.
Available everywhere as a how-to,
We'll find even ourselves in things all.

"Rejoice always, and in your faith delight."
"Be unceasing and in prayer persistent."
"In every situation be thankful all right."
And knowing what's in all things evident.

IN GARDENS OF DREAMS

Aria opens a beauty that brings

a blossoming rhapsody

And the joyous heart sings.

Its harmony, flourishing

the pleasure that springs

in Classical reposes

Of love in all themes.

Such are musical roses,

In gardens of dreams.

IN THREES

Zero is the expression of beginning as in

"at the start."

One is the expression of unity as in

"a coming toward."

Two is the expression of friendship as in

"heart to heart."

Three is the expression of harmony as in

"a common accord."

IS MY DREAM

Grace like a balm that soothingly restores

the aroma of lilies, savoring to the soul.

Inspiration like a wind that increasingly raises

the heights of imagination, enriching to the mind.

Nurturance like a song that harmoniously resonates

the lyrics of love, enthralling to the spirit.

Attractiveness like a painting that captivatingly romances

the visions of beauty, delighting to the heart.

IT'S ACRONYMIC

Harmful is the intent of the heart so moved.

Abhorrence is the inclined stand towards all.

Threatening is the impression so often proved

Enmity is the impact of such unrestrained gall.

Lacking what is necessary to continue its doing.

Exception that is negligible for it to be counted.

Subtracting what is nevermore to be practicing.

Smaller that is naturally the results amounted.

Liberally in an abundance of preserved passion.

Outpoured to an awaiting receptacle of the soul.

Valuing in an awareness of an exorbitant fashion.

Embraces to an appreciation of what's now whole.

Many can be organized as being the means to bless.

Others may be offered from the sources inside you.

Remaining can be obtained to use or even possess.

Extra may be ordained by God for Whom it's due.

IT'S UNFINISHED

He

was cast

adrift on the

sea of his delights,

as his heart set

sail for all

of her

charms.

LIFE

Today is the new beginning of a continuation.

Yesterday is the memory of all that proceeds.

Between them is the connection of continuity.

Tomorrow, then, is the awaiting of existence.

And I am the reservoir of hopes manifesting.

What are you and I, and all that is identified:

family members and others joined by experiences.

What was are the predecessors, ancestors, and histories.

What will be is the unseen, unlearned, and unknown.

And I am the dwelling of dreams and desires longing.

What I am in all of this are moments centrally figured;

to all that was, is, and will be; I am ever and always so.

Everything has its own starting and ending point,

for nothing can be ascertained without a now and when.

And I am primarily responsible for all of this: I am LIFE.

LIFE FORWARD

Winding down the Twenties' roaring,

Welcomed one with silent strength.

Wishing like all hope's a'soaring,

Wanted life's enduring length.

Making friends and times lasting,

Marked moments in pages kept.

Meaning like all promises casting,

Measured by each progress stepped.

Longing freedom, adulthood beckoning,

Listened a heart that's set aflight.

Loving like all desire reckoning,

Learned for the passages rite.

Raising child to maturity giving,

Remembered years in photos bound.

Recognizing like all worthy striving,

Realized the nobility of splendor crowned.

LOVE IN THE COLORS OF LIFE

ORANGE

... radiance of warmth and energy
surging like a beam of newly released light, giving over to a
flamboyance of fun and flights of fantasy in favored freedom.

YELLOW

... like the sun rising to dispel the loneliness of night,
a heart rises to the optimistic glow of
happiness establishing what is positively possible in its place.

BLUE

... the vastness of sky and ocean
invoking a calm restfulness of trust and dependability that
engenders commitment to a revisited heartfelt longing.

BROWN

... finding reliability of desire, once elusive
like that of a wind-swept promise, making
approachable what now captures the imagination.

(Continued on next page)

LOVE IN THE COLORS OF LIFE Cont.

PINK
... energy pulsating with the youthfulness of abandon,
desiring the mutual satisfactions of
sensuality's and passion's appetites.

RED
... emotions at the precipice of pleasurable wonders
and into the thralls of blissful elation, as
we're set adrift on roaring waves of romantic seas.

GREEN
... what naturally comes to a heart
tranquil as a softly moving stream, gently coursing its way
through moments of reflective thought in sublime silence.

GRAY
... wisdom as the maturing of knowledge,
the mind refining and dignifying what the body and soul
encounter, and the heart longs to embrace.

BLACK/WHITE
... sharply contrasted as right is to wrong, and yes is to no,
offerings of assurance in heart what
hope holds true: our lives being colored with love.

LOVE ON THE LINE

A smile, its beginning, this journey of delight.
A hope now inspiring a future that's bright.

May words now expressing a heart in its truth,
Lead to a revealing of affection for you.

In moments of sharing the love of our Lord,
Our faith ever growing as in one accord.

With joy overflowing, I pause to reflect
On God's will unfolding His path to direct.

Our friendship is blessing my life beyond measure,
To wit now confessing your soul I treasure.

Dear Lord, with thanksgiving, I ask you each day
For Love abiding in our hearts alway.

MAKING ME A WORLD

My hope as a world
where others find love and peace.

My heart as a place
where pain and fears cease.

My hands as the means
of being held with grace.

My home as the welcome
where all are one race.

MAYBE MAY BE

The easiest thing to say may be the worst way it is said.

The hardest thing to read may be the best thing ever read.

The quickest means to pay may be the costliest means paid.

The slowest means to make may be the surest means it's made.

The maybe may be more than a probability.

If maybe is much more than one can ever see.

The greatest way to win is the humblest way won.

The more may then begin once the maybe has begun.

MEMBER OF THE TEAMS: LIVING RESPONSIBLY

TEAM FAMILY

The team you're born into is the first to be joined.

If fortunate, it's complete with two parents, et al.

This isn't metaphorical, nor is it one cleverly coined.

It's your team for life, most deserving of your all.

TEAM WORKFORCE

The team you regularly report to on every work day.

The company has its own colors, there in its logo.

Your presence and performance are always on display.

The coaches and their bosses yelling: "Go-go-go!"

TEAM COMMUNITY

The team that supports it all is actually made of more.

It starts out with the neighborhood in which you live.

And guardians who willingly protect, serve, and restore.

What's more a church that uses whatever you can give.

TEAM YOU

The team that hasn't any players, except you and only you.

How often you pray, or well you play, it will be how long

You're able to be on your teams, but this you already knew.

Go fast, go slow, go far, go show, all it takes is to be strong.

MORE THAN MY VALENTINE

Times treasuring are passages to bliss.

Dreams becoming fulfilled by a design.

Hearts embracing what passions a kiss.

Plans joining lives together shall align.

Now professing adoration as to this:

Ever embracing more than my Valentine.

MY JEWEL

Virtue, as the passion of purity,

is the Magnificence of your soul.

Adoration, as the declaring of devotion,

is the Yearning of your spirit.

Nurture, as the promotion of promise,

is the Joy of your calling.

Excellence, as the aspiration of achievement,

is the Engagement of your will.

Service, as the height of humility,

is the Workmanship of your life.

Sophistication, as the cultivation of character,

is the Elegance of your manner.

Affection, as the tenderness of touch,

is the Loveliness of your heart.

NEVER SEVER

The meanings of most words are in their letters first.

In severity, it's something said or done to sever.

The manners being inflicted, who knows the worst?

In everlasting, this ends when its ever is never.

Everyone loses a great deal when these severings last.

Disconnections as lead-ins to disunity's divisiveness.

Disassociating will alienate, making each present a past.

Despite such disturbances, there's hope for distress.

Misunderstandings resolved when the ways are agreed.

Seeking the other's best makes things better for two.

And where harm has been done, go address that need.

Forgiving and forgetting will leave nothing to undo.

To never ever be severed cannot be promised anyone,

For problems will occur to challenge unity's accord.

Regardless of all this, we need never feel left all alone,

For we're never separated from God's love (the Lord).

OH, MY GOD

From my window, I could see so many smiles,

Happiness broadly displayed on countless faces.

I asked, why the distance as if so many miles?

Feeling captive regardless the location of places.

Alone I sat, with only a few companion thoughts.

Sensing your presence deep within my soul, I cried,

"I don't understand. So in doubt am I ... caught."

Waiting for an assurance, a still small voice replied.

"You've never been alone or ever out of my sight.

The sorrows you're feeling, those are mine as well.

To get rid of darkness, let this truth be as a light:

I've overcome the world, the one which you indwell.

So listen very closely, as this instruction is for you.

Don't just look at what's there, don't be missing out.

I've been out there all along, believe and it's true

That you'll know 'Oh, my God' is what it's all about."

114

OUR TIMES SUBLIME

Roses are red and violets are blue.
Sugar is sweet, and it is true

Rhymes are read as verses to bless.
Some will swoon upon their caress.

Hopes will lead all hearts to home.
Heaven is sent like in a tome.

Here we are for grace to seek.
Faith we live out while we speak.

Love thus grows within God's Way,
Led by Truth when we pray.

Thus, we'll see that all will be
More with you as well with me.

POETS' KNOWITS

To rhyme the time is to sublime the paradigm.

To write the light is to insight the bright.

To form the brainstorm is to transform the norm.

To verse the universe is to traverse the immerse.

To craft the draft is to engraft the aft.

To rhythm the whim is to metonym the hymn.

To lyric the empiric is to mesmeric the generic.

To pen the Zen is to stupend the yen.

PROTESTING IS PRO-TESTING

Protesting is the bane of freedom's existence.
When anger and hatred overflow constraints,
Then all sanity is sacrificed as a consequence,
And fear runs rampant with nary a complaint.

There are ways of causing protests to cease.
Fighting the wrong by promoting the right.
Preventing the violence by preserving the peace.
Exposing the darkness by shining truth's light.

Perspective is a means by which we can agree
That a protest is affirmation of a thing to test.
Whether to feign tolerance as in *fait accompli*,
Or strive with all resolve for what truly is best.

Don't be too quick in judging passions' pursuits,
For what seems wasteful is another's worthwhile.
And therein lies one of understanding's routes,
Due consideration be given for hearts to reconcile.

RAISE OF SONSHINE

Sunlight from the sky growing what could be
Our hopes planted like seeds, we wait to see.
Water, earth, and time bringing as they combine
To reap what is sown in the raise of Sonshine.

Conscious of what calls and demands for more
Ourselves being lifted higher than ever before.
Elevated to greater responsibilities we redefine
Processes by purpose from the raise of Sonshine.

Lines of succession are the pathways to progress.
Society becomes what all communities possess.
Therefore nurturing our futures is in our design,
Increasing potentials with every raise of Sonshine.

Moving forward throughout life it becomes known,
We travail, travel, and traverse though never alone.
With Divinely given grace for all things that are thine,
Going forward blessed is due to the raise of Sonshine.

REALITY IN SHADOWS

Obscure the one, and nothing of it is known.

Indistinct the image of imaginations become.

Faint the more, and partial is only shown.

Imperfect the idea of imitations therefrom.

Lose the certainty of presentable evidence.

Invisible the light of interceptions factual.

Vacate the capacity of representable subsequence.

Indelible the dark of inclinations actual.

RE-SOLVED

It's for me to do,
yet all I knew
was having lack
from what is due.

The passion's there,
yet much to share;
was offering how
from what or where.

I've found it thus,
yet all a fuss;
was needing change
from minus to plus.

Thank you indeed,
yet though in need;
will moving hence
from here to succeed.

SEEING HEARD – HEARING SEEN

I see what you mean.
You mean what you've seen.
I know what you show.
You show what you've known.

I get what you sought.
You sought what you've got.
I have what you add.
You add what you've had.

The more senses you use,
You're less likely to lose
The knowledge you gain,
Your memories will retain.

We see what we hear,
So lend me an ear
To hear what I see
Is what can again be.

SHE WON'T BE HOME
FOR CHRISTMAS

(The absence of a loved one recently deceased,
and the first Christmas celebrated without her.)

Busy were the days of preparations
for the saying of final goodbyes:
Arrangements made, songs sung,
tributes offered, and hugs shared.
Now begins what tasks delayed,
as shock gives in to weeping eyes,
The reality of an empty room,
and for whom Love manifestly cared.

Words fail me to describe the soul
whose presence still fills my thoughts.
Yet there's no comfort from giving voice
to reflections she left for me.
Her presents were wrapped as tradition dictates,
the always and the oughts,
But mom won't be home this Christmas,
for Christ wanted her with Thee.

SO LOVED (IS) THE WORLD

A familiar passage committed to memory first

Is the one which proclaims "For God so loves ..."

The truth of these words leaves a soul athirst

Our need of God is made aware from above.

"... the world that He gave ..."

Which begins answering the how of the why.

Those loved are souls whom He sought to save,

And of what He gave, nothing else could satisfy.

"... His only begotten Son."

God's love given in a most demonstrative fashion:

It was He in the person of Christ, the two as The One.

The earnestness of His love in such compelling passion.

(continued on next page)

123

SO LOVED (IS) THE WORLD Cont.

"… That whosoever believes in Him" reveals
The means by which God's love is known.
The void in everyone's heart invokes appeals
For what to believe of what has been shown.

"… should not perish but have everlasting life."
Speaks well of the power God's love commands.
This promise to all who believe makes hope rife
For what springs eternal in His extended hands.

The truths of this passage are meant for us all,
This love gift comes from the God of all glory.
And having thus received are faithful to the call
In offering His love through sharing of His story.

STAND THE KNEE WITH ME

I love my country; oh, yes, it's true,

And this is why I'm telling you.

A past so dark, yet now foreseen

A future bright, and a hope pristine.

We wield a power, and thus we'll stay

When stand the knee to bow and pray.

STANZAS OF LOVE

STANZA ONE

Oh, the sight of your radiant beauty.

Oh, the sound of your caressing voice.

Oh, the feel of your soothing touch.

Oh, the smell of your sweet fragrance.

Oh, the taste of your satisfying savor.

Taking all of you is in giving all of me.

STANZA TWO

My desire for you: have no want of anything.

My hope for you: know your purposes true.

My prayer for you: it is well with your soul.

My promise for you: be all I'm needed to be.

My gift for you: everything of mine as yours.

Being all for you as becoming all with me.

TALKING THE WALK

Tell me what you think.

Think of what I say.

Together we will talk

In truth along the way.

Show me what you know.

See by what I do.

Together we will walk

As with each other's view.

THE BUTTERFLY

Landing ever so lightly,
you generously touch the places your presence seems most welcoming.

Resting ever so peacefully,
you graciously spread your extraordinary beauty as I delight watching.

Looking ever so diligently,
you gratefully notice my strong gentle hand toward you now waiting.

Realizing ever so quickly,
you graciously respond to the offer of friendship I extend to you wishing.

Living ever so sincerely,
you gently bring with you inspired illumination, and I am left wanting.

Revealing ever so convincingly,
you gloriously exemplify Love, and I am enthralled worshipping.

THE DAWNING OF CHRISTMAS

'Twas the night after Christmas when throughout my heart,
All thoughts began stirring right from the start.

My awards had been hung on the mantle with care,
In the hope that someone would notice me there.

Their memories were nestled all snug in my mind,
While visions of glory diminished with time.

My friends having gone now and I left alone,
Had long settled down awaiting the phone.

When from the yard there arose such a clatter,
I sprang out of bed to check on the matter.

I ran to the doorway to see what I could,
And there was a present where someone once stood.

(Continued on next page)

THE DAWNING OF CHRISTMAS Cont.

I thought for a moment, "Oh, could it be,
Something special meant only for me?"

When what to my wondering eyes should appear,
But the following message, "For all to hear."

"By virgin birth He entered the world,
As the prophets foretold and at the angels' herald.

From 'In the beginning,' to, 'Behold His glory,'
So it was written, the true Christmas Story."

I stopped for a moment, amazed at myself.
"Haven't I read this before from my shelf?"

Yet, for some reason I had to proceed,
Out of some interest, but more so a need.

"Dressed in humanity from His head to His feet,
His clothes were swaddled, modest and neat.

(Continued on next page)

130

THE DAWNING OF CHRISTMAS Cont.

A treasure of gifts lay adorning His manger,
This infant Emmanuel, however a stranger.

"In wisdom and stature and favor He grew,
Before all mankind and the Father Who

Spoke of His pleasure in His Begotten Son,
A love so uniting that made them both one."

"Endued with all knowledge, understanding, and power,
To bring to God glory at a climactic hour.

In righteousness, holiness, justice, and love,
He faithfully lived out grace from above."

"He suffered rejection, betrayal, and deceit,
Even death on the cross, yet saw no defeat

(Continued on next page)

THE DAWNING OF CHRISTMAS Cont.

"Of His divine mission of salvation to bring,
To all people the gift of the King."

"So to you it is given this Holiday eve,
The most precious gift to freely receive.

By heartfelt belief and confession will He,
Be your Savior, Lord, and Life eternally."

"The Dawning of Christmas for all to hear
Are the words of Jesus, 'Salvation is near.'

The Dawning of Christmas for all to see,
Is Jesus the Christ in you and in me."

THE FLAG IDENTIFIES ME

For I'll kneel only to Thee

Except to pray that you see

Too much has already been said.

Were it left up to me

I would want us to be

United as one nation moving ahead.

To that end I promise you,

On my oath this I'll do

All that's good in God's sight.

And I pledge my allegiance true

To the red, white, and blue

Black, brown, red, yellow, and white.

THE HEARTS OF A MATTER

HEARING as the distinguishing of voices from the clamoring of noises;
What should matter most to you is listening for what's true.

ENTERTAINING as the deliberating of real from what holds no appeal;
What should matter most to be is what's really in it for me.

AFFIRMING as the declaring of conviction from any contradiction;
What does matter here is what conscience now makes clear.

RELATING as the discussing of perception from any misconception;
What does matter now is what self-disclosure you'll allow.

TRUSTING as the determining of mutual surety from any insecurity;
What will matter at this point is what foretells of joint.

SHARING as the demonstrating of charity from any insularity;
What will matter of these times is no longer what rhymes.

MATTERING as the disciplining of activity from any reactivity;
What makes a matter matter most is the heart it will host.

THE PASSING OF TIMES PAST

Quick the time remembered, a memory from then as now
... such were two souls' stories exchanged.

What destined the course, connection in summoned desire
... answers were curiosity's cravings arranged.

Long was the travel, the hours of minutes stretching far
... my mind wondering what "ifs" may be met.

Embarking on a tale untold, the prelude of nexts unfolding
... my body and yours in impassioned silhouette.

Freely the feelings opened, nakedness in all manners being
... my soul awakened to hidden truths uncovered.

Fragile our now becomes, the demands of nexts imposing
... my spirit alone again with self undiscovered.

THE SIGHS OF LIFE

"SM" may refer to try and to tire.
Perhaps it's to dream and to desire.

"M" is simply being exhausted,
or of commonly being inspired.

"L" makes greater the stress and the strain.
Likewise true of the growth and the gain.

"XL" profoundly increased is failing,
yet sweeter still is every prevailing.

THIS AS WE CHANGE

All who are here are here to see
If what's been said can truly be.
We come from old times known
To find new that's to be shown.

The call to change is oft unheard.
As if it's only a whispered word.
Change occurs at a point of need.
The heart will know and also heed.

When we've arrived, we start to feel
That what may happen to us is real.
In understanding what's been told.
These changes will naturally unfold.

With our new selves we can be sure
We're no longer whatever we were.
Of this one thing we can always rely.
For all of our needs God shall supply.

TO MY LADY

Laughter as music's sweetest sound,
Harmonizing my soul ...
(as she is amused by what also amuses me, and we laugh as one.)

Attraction as mankind's greatest delight
Uniting my heart...
(as she is the only woman with whom my heart desires to be.)

Dreams as creativity's fondest vision,
Inspiring my mind ...
(as she is the beauty that graces my thoughts, and I'm left undone.)

Yearning as love's strongest hope,
Motivating my being ...
(as she is inspirational in bringing out the best there is in me.)

TRUTH LIES

Swearing to tell what's true in whole and nothing but;
the witness to same is called upon to promise.

Bearing in mind that what's of an other not so another;
the record to show is conscience or compromise.

Impeding what's right is the pathway to falsity;
the verdict to render is denouncing what truth decries.

Informing what's wrong is the mainstay of honesty;
the oath to keep is finding where the truth lies.

TWO FOR ONE

I see people laughing and smiling with glee.
Enjoying everything that they see.
Having the times of their lives.
But I've absolutely nothing to smile about.
My life is very full of doubt.
Hoping what I am survives.

My friend is faced with much sadness and grief.
For him there's just no relief.
His problems won't go away.
Lord, I urgently need for him to see what I see.
That peace can be his with Thee.
Provide for this need I pray.

Friend, I'm reaching out to you, so take my hand.
Lean on me, and we will stand.
Trust me, and I will do you good.
[I know a way that you can help me.
Explain how much better my life can be.
Please show me if you would.]

(continued on next page)

TWO FOR ONE Cont.

Hear me. [I hear you.] God has a plan for your life.
He'll free you from your strife.
But you must repent and believe.
[Oh Lord. I know that I have sinned.
Forgive me, and with all my heart, I ask you in.
And your peace I gratefully receive.]

This poem you read is really a story.
Not about friends, but moreso God's glory.
Nothing is too little that's ever done.
It's in those moments when we offer our best.
God comes in and calls it blessed.
That's what happens with Two For One.

UNTO OTHERS AS ONESELF

It's familiar to do unto others as you would have them do to you.
It's said that such words can be likened to a Rule that is Golden.
It's understood that this is in relationship to loving in all ways true.
It's noteworthy that living this out requires more than an amen.

Being other-centered is the foundation of a life that gives to exceed.
Being self-centered is the sacrifice of a life that amounts to little.
Being God-centered is the consecration of a life that meets the need.
Being Biblically–centered is the assurance of a life becoming vital.

We're intricately connected in that what happens can affect all of us.
We're influenced by how others speak and act toward us in things.
We're interdependent in that actions do have consequences and thus
We're inspired by what is shared together with all that love brings.

VOWELS

"A" is the start of the alphabet and so much more.
This applies to everything, as long as it's afore.

"E" represents experiencing everyone and everything.
The question that ever arises is what to bring.

"I" represents the me as far as speaking for oneself.
Nothing so strange as that of an elf on a shelf.

"O" is the ending reached when all is said and done.
All that began has been from all that's begun.

"U" is the "you" of others addressed as if being seen.
What it comes down to is betwixt and between.

"Y" represents the promptings from within for answers.
Surprising, like this list, is when life then concurs.

WE ALL COME HERE

They're no longer here;

There where we once were.

And where we go from there,

Now is no longer clear.

They're where all are dear;

Here in all hearts near,

Wherein holds their tear,

As grief gives into cheer.

WE ARE THREE

Thee: God who created the earth, sky, and sea.
She: the one whose heart overflows with glee.
He: the one who personally desires hers to be.
We: the becoming one in the uniting of three.

Lifetimes are meaningful moments that grow
Desires and passions that compel us to know
What blessings that God now wills to bestow
In anointing us to further follow faith's flow.

The purpose for each life is for God to ordain
The process of believing in His love to retain
The promise guaranteed by Christ to remain
The prayers of hearts unto His glorious gain.

We reach for a future coming as He intends.
We service His pleasure as He so commends.
We willingly go wherever His love extends.
We live as if everything upon Him depends.

WHAT ALL REMAINS UNFINISHED

You proof your life as if in a class,
Reviewing your work before it's turned in.
"Why did I fail, or how do I pass?"
Needing to know is where you begin.

Expect from yourself the courage to ask,
Regarding what's done and what's left to do:
"Why wonder if I'm up to the task?"
Discovering in all things whatever is true.

Did you love too little, or perhaps too late,
Resolving in your mind you've plenty of time.
"Why should I; too busy; can't it just wait?"
Deciding to change for a better paradigm.

No longer will I leave well enough alone,
Reasoning that everything can be improved.
"Why did it take me so long to get here?"
Determining it's finished when what remains is best.

WHAT COUNTS OF A LIFE

Is it the number of successes toward fortune and fame,
Or the moments you prayerfully asked God to reclaim.
Is it the number of accolades you've received from afar,
Or the blessings from God who cares more how you are.

Could it be that all the riches coveted in life are fleeting,
Whereas the wealth from God's grace none can compare.
Could it be that the insatiability of prosperity is depleting,
Whereas the inexhaustibility of Providence wills declare.

Perhaps it's the perception one adopts in viewing reality,
Except that existence is never left to one's interpretation.
Perhaps it's a predetermination as inescapable causality.
Except that all things are possible with faith's foundation.

What counts for every single life is that which really counts
Before God Himself, as each one is judged as per His retell.
Like an historical recording that undeniably gives accounts
For how a life was truly lived, and for whom it was as well.

WHAT MAKES MANY ONE

EQUALITY

As in no one having any more rights than another.
That there is no difference in status of personhood.
Being like that of each other's sister and/or brother.
Opportunities afforded the same for all understood.

SOLIDARITY

As in the acknowledgment of common interests held.
The responsibility of our support requires each to give.
Being in full agreement over important issues dwelled.
Unity affirmed as the means by which we strive to live.

MUTUALITY

As in recognition of those personal feelings being shared.
The sense of obligation to one another is like a contract.
Being bound to another much like a partnership declared.
Interrelated and interdependent is therefore how all act.

IDENTITY

As in the close similarity of being whom and what we all are.
The discovery of commonness is what creates identification.
Being found linked and likened toward a becoming of an our.
Making the many one is by uniting together in celebration.

WORDS GONE WILD

I saw to see and seeing so,
I've seen what's sought by sight.
And said to say and saying said,
"It's must, or may, or might."

I think the thoughts as thought to think,
knowing known anew.
And find fine the finding found,
trusting Truth is truly true

AFTERWORD

Any story involving faith, which naturally produces hopes satisfied only in love, persists throughout time like that of a thread stitching together the tapestry of a life. The patterns and colors are as unique to the creation as are the qualities and characteristics of its creator. The collection of original poems you have just read are expressions of my life in words emanating from my heart to yours. This form of expression was intentionally used because it is the mode that best facilitates heart-to-heart communication.

The title of the book's final section, "Hearts Musing Life," was carefully chosen to reflect the meaningfulness of moments measured in time. The many poetic rhymes herein do not adequately give voice to all that living invites and introduces. Yet, the heart has a tremendous capacity to take in everything believed true and received new for meaning to be experienced with others.

We all have our own "Faith Hopes Love" stories to know and to show: our personal life's journey. It is my prayer that what you have of me adds both beauty and blessings beneficial to your life, and that what you take away from here is informative for what is yet to come.

— James "J.K." Sandin

APPENDIX A

A BRIDGE COVERS THEIR HEART expresses for me the feelings one has when carving names in a heart on the wall of a famed Madison County covered bridge: my parents as an example.

A CANDLE IN THE HEART expresses for me my thoughts about my mother captured in a poem framed with a candle in glass holder as a gift to her.

A CHILD YEARNS FOR WHAT A HEART RETURNS expresses for me the cries of a child in need and the hope that someone able to help will hear what only the heart can hear.

A MOTHER'S LOVE expresses for me the characteristics, qualities, and nature of a mother's love.

A SPECIAL SOMEONE expresses for me God's love demonstrated through His providing someone special into another person's life, especially in a time of need for love to be shown him or her.

A TEACHER NEVER RETIRES expresses for me my thoughts about my sister captured in a poem as a gift in celebration of her retirement from teaching.

A TEACHER'S PRAYER expresses for me my thoughts about my sister's heartfelt commitment to her young charges while teaching, as well as in retirement.

ADDING CHANGES expresses for me a truth that adding something here and/or something there does change the meaning of a word or message.

ALL THINGS BE expresses for me a personal desire to be who and what I need to be for myself, and that which is needed of me by others.

ALWAYS expresses for me a satisfaction so great that it prompts an exaltation of its Source as the soul is surrendered to its Savior.

AN END'S BEGINNING expresses for me an exercise in playing with words to mean the same thing when read forward as they do being read backwards.

AS IS MY LADY TO ME expresses my admiration and love for a woman with whom I was engaged, and for whom I would do and be anything.

AT LONG LAST LOVERS expresses for me what I thought I was experiencing until I awoke.

BEING AND BECOMING expresses for me the thought that to be, one must be becoming, and that through experiencing what brings about being.

BEING GOOD FOR BETTER TO BEST expresses for me the fact that life is progressive, from being to seeking, and from finding to sharing for the good, best, and betterment of all.

BUT WE SEE JESUS expresses for me the truth that, in the midst of crises, we can and must see Jesus.

CHRISTMAS DAWNS expresses for me the sincere search of a soul longing for a truth that transcends the trite and traditional as the Light of Christ dawns within. (Sequel to "The Dawning of Christmas.")

COME-UNITY expresses for me the efforts it takes to create a sense of community beneficial to all.

COMING ATTRACTIONS – LIFE ON THE REAL SCREEN expresses for me how our own lives are written, directed, produced, and starring ourselves, viewed by others in the theaters of our respective worlds.

CONFUSION'S INTRUSIONS expresses for me how confusion intrudes upon one's life (i.e., relationships, peace), and what steps to take in either resolving or even precluding them.

CONTEXTING expresses for me the fun of learning and using a new language like that used in texting.

DAD RHYMES WITH expresses for me an acknowledging and appreciating of the qualities and characteristics that make one's dad a rhyme with him as a focus of one's life.

DAWNINGS OF AGO expresses for me how the experiences of the past permeate the present.

EVER VALENTINES expresses for me what I would desire to experience with my Valentine for life, that being a perfect match in complementarity.

FAITH, HOPE, AND LOVE: A POEM expresses for me the thought that these three virtues are our best teachers of truth, provided we prayerfully and proactively pursue them in our daily lives.

FAMILY TIES expresses for me what I've always known, that family ties everything together in life.

FLOWING expresses for me what the experience is like to be in the flow of love welling up within my heart for someone I desire.

FROM A MAN'S DESIRE ... OF A WOMAN'S HEART expresses for me the requisites for a man who desires the heart of a woman and what a woman's heart requires of her man.

GIVING VOICE TO GLORY expresses for me who I am in response to who Christ Jesus is to me and the effect He has on my soul and in my life.

GOODBYES BY GOOD expresses for me that saying goodbye is not an end in itself, but an ushering in of new beginnings that bring with them the potential for good to come.

GROOMING TO BLOOMING expresses for me how life experiences serve to prepare us for the blooming of potential long awaited for, and surpassing expectations by the grace of God.

HELLO GOODBYES expresses for me a welcoming of what ends in life to let something new arise.

HER WORDS MY SOUL'S CARESS expresses for me what I felt whenever I spoke with a woman of my heart's pleasure during a stressful time in the pursuit of an opportunity.

HERE expresses for me the human obsession with both the past and future, at the exclusion of considering the only time period one can readily experience and change: "now."

I AM expresses for me the self-awareness, self-determination, and self-affirmation that are habits and stands that I strongly advocate and regularly practice.

IN ALL THINGS expresses for me that there is much to discover in everything that always leaves room for being all the more curious and all the more thankful for what is found.

IN GARDENS OF DREAMS expresses for me a connection between music in one's soul accompanying the dreams in one's mind; and the poem began as a song.

IN THREES expresses for me the impressionistic importance of numbers as combinations innately contributing to life.

IN WANT I WONDER (PART 1) expresses for me personal lessons being learned about getting past the past, and looking confidently at self now in light of future.

IN WANT I WONDER (PART 2) expresses for me metaphorically the experience of a desire for a love being fulfilled, and the desire for Love ever increasing.

IN WANT OF NOTHING expresses for me a profession of faith that is borne out of personal experiences firmly forming said beliefs.

IS MY DREAM expresses for me the feelings I had in meeting someone likened to my fondest dreams.

IT'S ACRONYMIC expresses for me how applying deeper meaning to words reveals what they actually spell out for us when fully taken into consideration.

IT'S UNFINISHED expresses for me faith hoping for love to the point of taking action for the heart's cause, and that not everything in life is completed.

LIFE expresses for me the height, depth, and breath of all that was, of all that is, and all that ever shall be in our individual and collective existence.

LIFE FORWARD expresses for me the life of my mother, which I attempted to capture poetically in a poem gifted to her on her birthday.

LIKE THIS IS THAT expresses for me a time when I was metaphorically musing about life in a moment of deep reflection.

LOVE FOLLOWS THE LONGING HEART expresses for me the desire, determination, and delight in the promise, pursuit, and pleasure of love.

LOVE IN THE COLORS OF LIFE expresses for me the coloration of the feelings I associate with the experiences of love at all levels and in all facets.

LOVE IS ... expresses for me the images and experiences I associate with love as best I could express in response to a question posed to me.

LOVE ON THE LINE expresses for me a profession of faith about someone dear to me, and a prayer of thanks to God for that same dear person.

MAKING ME A WORLD expresses for me a responsibility to my fellow person for loving her/him in ways that are meaningful for her/his betterment.

MAYBE MAY BE expresses for me a belief that in the existence of possibilities and probabilities is the ever present hope for more than maybe.

MEMBER OF THE TEAMS expresses for me the fact that we all are members of some very special teams, and the fulfillment of our respective responsibilities will determine how strong we are in them.

MORE THAN MY VALENTINE expresses for me what I would like to read in a Valentine and give that same card to the one whom my heart desires to have as same.

MUSICAL ROSES: ALL THAT SUPPOSES expresses for me my attempt at describing what I hear and see musically when in love, in answer to a question once posed to me.

MY HEART ALL WAYS expresses for me what a heart may and ought to be in all ways always for all.

MY JEWEL expresses for me the strong feelings I had for the woman who called me her Gem and whose name appears in the poem.

MY LOVE IS ... expresses for me who my dreamed love would be described by me in simile fashion, as if she could be as so described.

MY LOVE IS HOME expresses for me what it means when someone is at home in my heart, and she has subsequently become home for me.

MY THOUGHTS OF YOU expresses what I anticipated in a trip to meet someone for whom my heart desired, and the eventual experience of meeting her.

NEVER SEVER expresses for me the importance and blessings of remaining connected to one another, especially in light of the fact that nothing can ever separate (sever) us from God's love for one and all.

OH, MY GOD expresses for me the reaction a person might have when realizing that he/she was never alone in times of loneliness or despair, for God was with him/her all the time and in every way.

OUR JOURNEY AND AMEN (DESIRING) expresses what I felt for a special woman with whom I had become emotionally connected and had responded to her heart's calling.

OUR JOURNEY FROM THEN (CONNECTING) expresses what I experienced in the actual process of feeling connected with a special woman whom my heart desired.

OUR JOURNEY FROM WHEN (SUMMONING) expresses what I experienced with a special woman of feeling drawn to her as my heart was responding to her heart bidding me come.

OUR LOVE IS LIKE expresses for me the effects the idealized love of my life would have on me.

OUR TIMES SUBLIME expresses for me what I continue to experience with a woman who has my heart in her for now and for all eternity, as Love makes known to us a life blessed for all time.

POETS' KNOWITS expresses for me a whimsical look at poetry from a playfully poetic point of view.

PROTESTING IS PRO-TESTING expresses for me the positive value of protesting when it is conducted with pure motivations expressed in civil tones and actions, rather than in negative riotous incivility.

RAISE OF SONSHINE expresses for me how God elevates life to higher levels of experience and standards of excellence so long as we receive the blessings He continually pours out through His Son.

REALITY IN SHADOWS expresses for me the impossibility of confidence when all that could otherwise be seen is in darkness.

RE-SOLVED expresses for me what I was feeling during a period of reflection in a depressed state of mind trying to lift myself out of same.

SEEING HEARD – HEARING SEEN expresses for me the flexibility of our senses when used creatively.

SHE WON'T BE HOME FOR CHRISTMAS expresses for me the thoughts and feelings I experienced as I celebrated my first Christmas holiday without my mom's gracing presence.

SO LOVED (IS) THE WORLD expresses to me the fact that God's love is so universally personal that it is offered to the individual through Christ to the point of all-inclusively embracing the world in Him.

STAND THE KNEE WITH ME expresses for me the fact that the greatness of America is established and sustained through prayer corporately agreed upon, which God promises to always answer.

STANZAS OF LOVE expresses for me what I experience when in love with someone, and the lengths to which I'm willing to go in demonstrably proving it so.

TALKING THE WALK expresses for me how to communicate openly in mind and heart, which was actually the jingle of my web show of the same name.

THAT I MAY KNOW expresses for me the truth that to really know something, one must go through a process of learning through experience for it.

THE BUTTERFLY expresses for me metaphorically my thoughts of a woman whose friendship is precious to me, and who loves purple butterflies.

THE DAWNING OF CHRISTMAS expresses for me an alternative viewpoint of celebrating the Christ of Christmas in light of the secularized story that ignores the true meaning of the Holiday completely.

THE FLAG IDENTIFIES ME expresses for me what pledging allegiance means beyond the oath of words.

THE "HEARTS" OF A MATTER expresses for me how hearing and entertaining faith, affirming and relating hopes, and trusting and sharing love are the processes of life regarding every matter.

THE PASSING OF TIMES PAST expresses for me the loss of a relationship that once overflowed with hope, yet ended before the love did in my heart for her.

THE SIGHS OF LIFE expresses for me the depths of determined effort that increases with the size of the task.

THE WAYS TO YOU expresses for me metaphorically the ways to approaching a love (person) and the ways to discovering Love (God in Christ Jesus).

THINKING OF YOU expresses my feelings for a woman I had the pleasure of romancing, the name of whom appears in the poem.

THIS AS WE CHANGE expresses for me the process of change that is universally experienced, but is seldom appreciated or affirmed, and that it's good to look at this again from a fresh perspective.

TO MY LADY expresses for me who my dreamed-about lady is to me, and this is a dream I hope by faith becomes a living, loving reality.

TOGETHERING expresses for me what it means to be with someone in life as in sharing life together.

TRUTH LIES expresses for me what belies the truth, and where it (truth) will always be found.

TWO FOR ONE expresses for me in storytelling form how, especially for a person of faith, helping a friend in need is never an action undertaken completely alone, as God is very much involved in this.

UNTO OTHERS AS ONESELF expresses for me how closely connected we are to one another, to the point where what is said or done affects both parties and how that should give us all pause.

VOWELS expresses for me a simplification of life into six representational letters used every day.

WE ALL COME HERE expresses for me the very personal yet universal process of grieving death.

WE ARE THREE expresses for me the spiritual reality of a relationship between a man and a woman whose faith in the Lord is central, welcoming Him in everything they say and do as always being three.

WHAT ALL REMAINS UNFINISHED expresses for me how to become reconciled to life at its end.

WHAT COMES OF HOPE expresses for me how to describe the search for and experience of hope.

WHAT COUNTS OF A LIFE expresses for me the things that are most important in one's life compared to what may otherwise be accepted for lack of counting the cost of one's decisions.

WHAT MAKES MANY ONE expresses for me the means by which two or more people, as different as they may be, may still find reasons to emphasize their (our) commonalities and become as one People.

WHEN COMES TWO HEARTS IN ONE expresses for me what a man feels as he anticipates becoming one with the woman his heart desires.

WHY … expresses for me the most important questions we collectively face in life and my attempt at poetically trying to answer these same questions.

WORDS GONE WILD expresses for me an important fact of life, that truth can always be trusted.

YESTERDAYS' TOMORROWS expresses for me my hopes and thoughts for each new today, having seen the previous ones become past.

APPENDIX B

HEARTS HEARING ...

Faith is shown kneeling before an opened Bible while she is "hearing."

HEARTS ENTERTAINING ...

Faith is shown journaling her inspirational thoughts as "entertained."

HEARTS AFFIRMING ...

Faith is shown amidst beauty with her hopes, as hands are raised "affirming."

HEARTS RELATING ...

Faith is shown reaching out to those around in her hopes of "relating."

HEARTS TRUSTING ...

Faith is shown stretching forth her heart as if in her hands "trusting."

HEARTS SHARING ...

Faith is shown holding hands with others of hoped for love now "sharing."

HEARTS MUSING ...

Faith Hopes Love prompts thoughtfulness of life voiced in verses "musing."

INDEX

161

163

MEET THE AUTHOR

JAMES "J.K." SANDIN

J.K. has been writing poetry for decades, ever since his first piece received favorable response from a holiday talent show audience in 1985. The piece was titled *The Dawning of Christmas* and was inspired by Clement Clarke Moore's classic, *A Visit From Saint Nicholas*. *Faith Hopes Love* represents J.K.'s entry into the literary world, and he has many more works in process at the present time.

J.K.'s academic training is in the communication arts. He professionally identifies himself as an interpersonal communications specialist. As the Founder and Owner of a communication consultancy (Speak With EEEs, LLC), J.K. serves by helping to empower the messenger and enhance the message in order to more effectively reach targeted audiences and markets and to outstand their brand.

Meaningfully contributing to the betterment of others is what makes J.K. the passionate person he is. The spirit of his writings is the content of his soul: love for the truth. And what gives him the greatest pleasure as a writer is the satisfaction his readers derive from receiving what is in his heart for them: the best he has to give for the best which they can live.

MEET THE ARTIST

GRACE METZGER-FORREST

After the Art Institute, Grace started animating children's CDs for a company called Knowledge Engineering in the Buckhead area of Atlanta. At Appletree Technologies, which became a New Horizon Training Center, she worked for their Multimedia Division.

From there she drove to DayStar Digital on the outskirts of Atlanta where she worked in Director on an interface for their product line CD, which won a New Media Invision Bronze. She also illustrated products and enhanced photos.

As a freelancer, Grace worked for a lot of different clients on many different types of projects: animated mutating cells for the CDC, internal presentations in the basement of the Coca-Cola Corporation, created scenes for a video game (don't ask), morphed Jell-o creations into Jell-o creatures for a Cartoon Network screensaver.

Currently, she creates in a small studio in the top of her house in a little town on the Chesapeake Bay. When not working, Grace likes to sketch portraits in oil pastel or create detailed, shaded drawings in pencil. She shares a "junior" farm, as they call it, with her husband and daughter, complete with a garden, three chickens, and a goat.

The LOVE chart on the next page is designed to be cut from this book and framed or posted on a refrigerator, mirror, desk, or any other prominent place as a reminder to always live in love. You may also download a color version suitable for printing and framing from the **Faith Hopes Love** book page at: www.TheLaurusCompany.com

LOVE IS
patient • kind

LOVE DOES NOT
envy • boast • dishonor others

LOVE IS NOT
proud • self-seeking • easily angered

LOVE KEEPS
no record of wrongs

LOVE DOES
not delight in evil • rejoice with the truth

LOVE ALWAYS
protects • trusts • hopes • perseveres

LOVE NEVER FAILS!

1 Corinthians 13:4-8

CPSIA information can be obtained
at www.ICGtesting.com
Printed in the USA
FFHW010413050119
50017423-54771FF